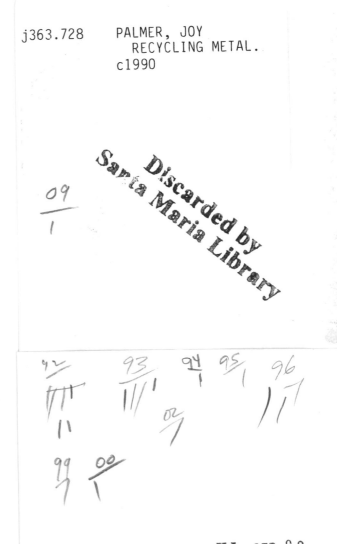

© Franklin Watts 1990

Franklin Watts Inc
387 Park Avenue South
New York
NY 10016

Printed in Belgium

Editor
Ruth Taylor

Picture researcher
Sarah Ridley

Designed by
Sally Boothroyd

Illustrations by
Tony Kenyon
Raymond Turvey
Matthew White

Photographs
Courtesy of Alcan Aluminium Can Recycling page 17(B); Dennis Barnes 23(L); courtesy of British Steel Tinplate 19, 28; Ecoscene 8, 10, 20, 27; Eye Ubiquitous 13(T), 13(B), 18; Chris Fairclough Colour Library 16; Hutchison Library 23(R); courtesy of International Tin Research Institute 15, 21; Maggie Murray/Format 9; Brenda Prince/Format 6-7; courtesy of Reynolds Aluminum 17(T); ZEFA 11.

Library of Congress Cataloging-in-Publication Data

Palmer, Joy.
  Recycling metal / Joy Palmer.
    p.   cm. — (Waste control)
  Summary: Explains the environmental problems that result from the manufacture and disposal of everyday items made of metal and shows how the recycling of these objects can reduce these threats.
    ISBN 0-531-14118-7
    1. Scrap metals–Recycling–Juvenile literature. 2. Scrap metals–Environmental aspects–Juvenile literature. [1. Scrap metals–Recycling. 2. Scrap metals–Environmental aspects. 3. Recycling (Waste) 4. Refuse and refuse disposal.] I. Title. II. Series. Palmer, Joy. Waste control.
  TD799.5.P34 1991
  363.72'8—dc20   90-32530
                                          CIP   AC

Recycling METAL

Joy Palmer

Franklin Watts

New York/London/Toronto/Sydney

CONTENTS

Throughout the world, metal is collected for recycling. This heap of cans has been sorted at a garbage dump at Smokey Mountain in the Philippines.

INTRODUCTION

The word *waste* means something that is left over after use, superfluous and no longer serving a purpose. For a long time people have been in the habit of throwing away such materials, believing that they no longer have value. Indeed, we live in a throwaway society and it can be all too easy to discard leftovers into a garbage can to be collected and disposed of. Most wastes, however, are far too valuable to throw away. Metal waste, whether from household or industry, certainly falls into this category.

Metal is one of the four main ingredients of domestic waste, the others being organic matter (such as food scraps), paper, and glass. In total, metals make up around 9 percent by weight of household leftovers.

There are various ways to deal with waste: for example, it may be buried in the ground or burned. Whatever we do with waste, it cannot just disappear from the world as if by magic. Buried waste may be out of sight – but it is a potential source of problems, for example, the leaking of poisonous substances into the soil. The incineration of waste may also be problematic – perhaps gas and smoke will be released to pollute the air we breathe. Without doubt, waste must be controlled and managed efficiently. The best possible solution is to recycle waste, that is, to reclaim it and reuse it, perhaps in a different form.

The topic of metals is vast; so the limited space available here is used to concentrate on those metals most commonly found in our own waste, namely iron/steel, aluminum and tin.

METALS TO WASTE?

Waste metal comes from both household and industrial sources. In the United States, by weight, metals account for around 9 percent of the total domestic waste. An inspection of the "average" family garbage can will no doubt reveal a vast assortment of cans that once contained items ranging from cola to corn and soup to sausages. Over 70 billion metal food and drink cans are purchased every year. Taking the national average, each person uses one can every day.

Such amazingly high figures illustrate what a remarkable amount of aluminum, tin, and steel is regularly tossed into the waste disposal stream of the nation. Yet far from being superfluous junk, these cans can be reclaimed and recycled, allowing their metals to be put to good further use.

On a larger scale, the reclamation of metals such as iron and steel is vital, both to the economy of our own nation and to the world as a whole. It is a major industry in its own right, yet one in which we can all participate. In the United States, the Institute of Scrap Recycling Industries represents the scrap metal dealers and processors who supply the scrap metal requirements of the steel industry.

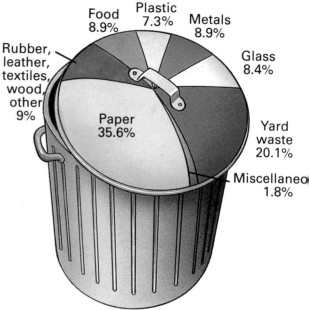

Food 8.9%
Plastic 7.3%
Metals 8.9%
Glass 8.4%
Rubber, leather, textiles, wood, other 9%
Paper 35.6%
Yard waste 20.1%
Miscellaneo 1.8%

Metals make up 9 percent of household waste. (Figures from United States Environmental Protection Agency.)

Household metal – junk or valued? This container holds a wide range of items discarded from the home that are a valuable source of metal scrap.

We live in a throwaway age and it is all too easy to dispose of scrap metal in a thoughtless way. Small items are frequently tossed into the wastebasket when they could well be sorted and reclaimed for scrap. Larger items are even more problematic. This car has been abandoned. Not only would it have value as scrap metal. It is also spoiling the beauty of the landscape.

Recycling begins at home. From time to time every household considers how to dispose of unwanted items such as an old refrigerator, washing machine or bicycle, all of which are valuable for recycling back into the metal industry.

Recycling enables vital supplies of the world's raw materials to be saved. It also reduces the need to transport materials to processing plants. Metal recycling saves energy too: making steel from scrap uses approximately one-quarter of the energy needed to convert raw iron ore into steel; recycling aluminum uses only 5 percent of the energy required to make aluminum from bauxite. Anyone interested in conservation and the quality of our environment will appreciate such advantages associated with the use of recycled scrap metal. Recycling causes far less pollution of the air, water, and soil, and it does not use the large amounts of water that are required when steel is produced from raw materials.

All of these ideas are elaborated upon in the forthcoming pages, but at this stage one key fact should be emphasized: a much larger proportion of the world's waste must be recycled, a task which should be of concern to every individual. Recycling begins at

home, and without doubt SCRAP METAL = WEALTH. The remainder of this book takes a more detailed look at certain metals, their uses and possibilities for recycling. It outlines case studies of good practice and, more importantly, suggests ways in which more people may become involved in this action.

RECYCLE!

SAVE RAW MATERIALS

SAVE MONEY

SAVE ENERGY

SAVE WATER – REDUCE POLLUTION

THE IRON AND STEEL INDUSTRY

This blast furnace is for making iron. It is situated at Redcar, Teesside, and is the largest in Europe. It is operated by British Steel.

Iron is the world's most used metal. A mineral called iron ore, together with coal and limestone are the three key raw materials needed for making it. In turn, iron can be transformed into steel.

A large construction known as a blast furnace is used for making iron. Within this huge oven, coals are heated for many hours. The raw materials of coke (coals), ore, and limestone are fed in through the top of the furnace. At the same time, air, heated to an extremely high temperature, is forced under high pressure into part of the furnace known as the melting zone. The hot air enables the coke to burn fiercely, so that great heat and a large amount of gas are produced. This is carried upward to an outlet near the top of the furnace. The gas reacts with the ore and other raw materials to produce a substance called metallic iron, which melts and is carried down to the bottom of the furnace. While this is happening, the limestone mixes with impurities in the ore and coke to form molten slag which settles on top of the iron. This process continues uninterrupted, and the slag and metallic iron are "run off," or removed separately, through outlets in the base of the furnace. The metallic iron can then be transferred elsewhere to be made into steel. Most of the impurities in the iron (for example, silicon, sulfur, phosphorus) are removed and the amount of carbon it contains is reduced.

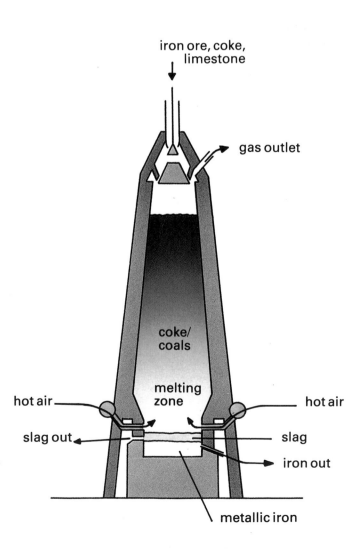

The workings of a blast furnace.

The iron may be dealt with in a number of ways, perhaps in a Basic Oxygen Converter. This device can tilt forward and backward. First, some scrap steel is put into it, followed by the molten iron. A long tube then pipes oxygen into the converter and onto the surface of the iron. This results in a chemical change so that impurities are removed and the iron is transformed into molten steel. The molten steel is poured out of the converter into special molds where it cools and becomes solid, creating blocks of metal known as steel ingots.

The ingots may be heated, rolled into thinner strips and cut into lengths called slabs. These are then cooled and inspected before being heated once again. The reheated metal enters a hot strip-mill, where it is reduced in thickness until it becomes a coil of thin steel or sheet that can be sold to industrial customers.

This whole process is dependent on the mineral iron ore. Like all other minerals found on our earth, iron ore is a finite, non-renewable resource – in other words, if we use it all up it is gone forever. Known reserves, from which iron may be extracted, are unevenly distributed in the crust of the earth. It is difficult to predict the consumption of minerals and to estimate how long reserves will last. At the time of writing iron is in good supply, yet some scientists are pessimistic. In the United States good-quality iron deposits in Minnesota and Michigan have been badly depleted and the proportion of imported ore is increasing. It has been estimated that the life expectancy of iron ore may be only 100 – 200 years. Without doubt, efforts must be made to conserve resources: one major way to achieve this is through successful recycling of iron and steel.

A basic oxygen converter. Molten steel can be poured out of the converter into molds.

Steelmaking takes place in a similar way throughout the world. This blast furnace is transforming iron into steel in Argentina.

ANY OLD IRON AND STEEL?

Reclamation of iron and steel is vital for the conservation of Earth's finite resources and to the economy of individual nations and the world as a whole. It is a major industry in its own right. In the United States the Institute of Scrap Recycling Industries represents some 1,750 scrap dealers and processors, who share the task of supplying the scrap requirements of the steel industry.

Waste material for reclamation and recycling comes from three main sources. First, there are large scrap-producing industries from which regular collections are made. Second, much is derived from the demolition and dismantling of buildings and equipment constructed from metal. Third, there are scavengers who seek out scrap metal to sell to dealers.

The American scrap metal industry probably ranks as one of the best equipped and most efficient and competitive in the world. More capital investment has gone into it in recent years than into almost any other industry. All scrap collected is sorted, graded and processed before being delivered in bulk to steelmakers and foundries for recycling.

It costs around $2.5 million to set up a medium-sized scrap-processing plant. In 1928, when the Scrap Institute was established, hammers, hacksaws, hand-held shears and chisels were the tools used for breaking up metal; strong men with shovels and forks, aided by horses and carts, would move it about. Today, a well-equipped processing plant contains "hydraulic shears," "shredders," and "balers" which break, cut, shred, and then bale the metal for its return to the steel industry. It must be stressed that not only iron, but large amounts of nonferrous scrap (i.e., not containing iron) are recovered at the same time. Many processing plants have departments dealing with nonferrous metals such as copper, lead, and brass, since these are also valuable materials for recycling.

Scrap metal derives from three sources. These are the large scrap-producing industries, the dismantling of buildings, and the "small," itinerant collectors of junk metal.

All scrap is sorted, graded and processed before being delivered to the steel industry. This scrap has passed through the first stages of recovery and is waiting for shredding and cutting.

After it has been broken up and shredded, the metal is then baled so that it can be returned to the steelmakers for reuse.

Scrap processing is a vital industry for economic and environmental reasons. At present, almost 50 percent of the steel in the United States and virtually all the cast iron and refined iron are made from scrap metal. Without this, we would have to spend hundreds of millions of dollars on importing additional raw materials. Recycling metal saves energy, conserves water and finite mineral reserves, and reduces air pollution. Worldwide, the heavy steel industry uses scrap for some 50 percent of its iron requirements. The United States is the world's leading nation in the scrap business, where 35 percent of heavy metals are recycled. Most of this material comes from used machinery, transport, and construction materials. In 1989 the United States exported around 13 million tons of iron and steel scrap. However, in many nations and indeed globally, there is much room for improvement in recycling efforts.

At this shredding plant the disintegrated and sorted metal awaits baling. Today these processes are carried out with the aid of modern machinery – a far cry from the early days of reclamation when men used hacksaws and chisels for the task!

FOOD CANS: THE GOOD, THE BAD AND THE UGLY

Over 70 billion cans are purchased in the United States every year – and that figure is constantly rising! Worldwide, most cans are made from either tinplate or aluminum or a combination of the two metals. Tinplate is a sheet of high-quality steel coated with very fine layers of pure tin. The tin protects the can from corrosion.

Food cans have been around for almost 200 years. In 1795 Napoleon offered a prize to anyone who could find a method of preserving food for the soldiers in his armies. The prize was won in 1810 by a Frenchman who did interesting work in sterilizing food. In the same year, an Englishman named Peter Durand designed a tin-plated iron can that would act as a food container. All of these early cans were made of iron and coated with a thin layer of tin. Manufacturers could make 60 of them in a day.

Since then, numerous developments and inventions have revolutionized the canning industry. In 1890, the first automatic can-making machinery was introduced in Britain. In 1935, beer came in cans for the first time. In 1963 the ring-pull aluminum can was invented, and in 1964 manufacturers in the United States developed a can made only of two pieces of aluminum. The first tin-free steel cans were made in Britain in 1968. Modern can-making factories produce over 1,000,000 cans a day compared to the 60 of 1810!

Canned foods are extremely convenient. With a store of canned foods in your kitchen, you can produce a meal easily, even if the grocery stores are closed. Canned foods have already been prepared and cooked, and so need only to be reheated before serving: this saves time and effort. Canned food is good

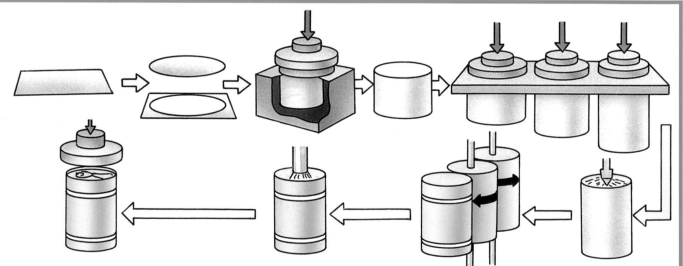

How a two-piece drink can is made. A circle is stamped out of an aluminum sheet and then pressed into a mold to make a cylindrical container about half the height that the can will be when it is finished. This container is further pressed, or stamped, so that the sides become thinner and taller, but the base remains thicker. The inside of the can is sprayed, to prevent the contents from being contaminated, and the outside is printed. The can is filled with drink and an aluminum ring-pull lid is sealed on top.

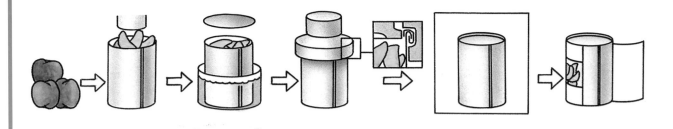

Canning. Fresh food is cleaned, prepared and blanched and put into sterile cans, together with some liquid. The cans are heated in hot water, to remove air, and then sealed. Next the cans are heated in a steam-pressure container, to make the contents sterile, and finally the labels are added.

quality because only first-class foods are selected for canning and no artificial preservatives are added: it is the actual cooking and canning process which preserves the food. Food in cans lasts a long time if kept in a cool, dry place. It does not need to take up space in a refrigerator. Similar advantages could be listed for canned drinks.

Unfortunately, the value of cans is offset by some bad and ugly aspects of their use. Cans and ring-pulls are tossed aside as litter, spoiling our environment and creating hazardous waste. Many birds and animals die each year, cut by the rough edges of broken cans or by swallowing ring-pulls.

The answer, of course, is recycling. An aluminum can thrown out of a car window could still be littering the earth in 500 years' time. One aluminum can recycled saves energy equivalent to that needed to operate your television set for three hours.

All of the general economic and ecological arguments put forward in favor of heavy metal recycling obviously hold true for cans, which, indeed, form part of the scrap metal industry. Can recycling helps to preserve the earth's finite resources. It saves money, energy, and materials, and reduces the volume of solid waste. Furthermore, it helps to prevent our world being spoiled by hazardous and unsightly litter.

Two-piece drink cans leaving a can-making line.

STEEL CANS: TIN AND BIMETAL RECYCLING

Tin cans are made of steel, with a thin coating of tin to prevent corrosion of the steel. Bimetal cans are tin-coated steel with one or both ends made of aluminum. Many drink cans are tin-plated steel with an aluminum top and ring-pull. Recycling these cans is much more difficult than recycling all-aluminum ones.

About 300,000 tons of steel cans are recycled in the United States each year. This total includes drink cans, as well as food, petfood and aerosol cans. While much emphasis is put on encouraging the public to recycle drink cans, these actually form only a small part of the steel recycling potential.

Steel cans are reclaimed for recycling in two ways. They can be collected by means of local recycling programs, in which people separate their used cans into a special bin for curbside pickup or take them to a special collection center. Otherwise, steel cans can be separated from household waste after it has been collected by the local sanitation authority. In Collier County, Florida, for example, the county's department of Solid Waste mines its landfill for materials to be recycled. In this program, ferrous metals and aluminum are separated and provided to recycling industries.

Save-a-Can programs are an important element of recycling initiatives in the United Kingdom. Consumers are encouraged to take along used steel cans and deposit them in a bin. The number of Save-a-Can sites is increasing.

Food cans, petfood cans, aerosol cans — any family's regular shopping trip to the supermarket will probably result in a wide variety of cans being purchased.

Used steel cans are collected at waste processing plants using a magnetized conveyor belt.

Thousands of steel cans can be collected at waste disposal incinerators by means of large electromagnets and used to make new steel products.

Where waste is burned, steel cans are sometimes removed before the rest of the waste is incinerated, and sometimes the metal is extracted after incineration. In the latter case, the metal is returned for re-use. Cans extracted from waste that has not been incinerated are processed to remove any tin and leave very good-quality scrap steel. Incinerated cans do not need this detinning treatment before they can be remelted in the steelworks, but cannot be recycled into a high-quality product.

Steel from cans forms only a tiny part of the total scrap steel derived from industrial nations, but its potential must not be underestimated. Every contribution at a local level forms part of a partnership between individuals and industry that will have some impact on global metal conservation.

THE CAN MAKERS: COOPERATION FOR RECYCLING

If any substantial progress is to be made in recycling, then partnership and cooperation are essential. The Aluminum Recycling Association is dedicated to conserving energy and preserving raw materials. Its members work closely with the National Soft Drink Association to promote good management of resources and recycling of metals.

Recent attention to the quantity of resources used has led to a dramatic reduction in the materials needed for making cans. Can walls are now made thinner, in a process known as lightweighting. In 1970 a typical soft drink can weighed 2 ounces (57g); it now weighs 1¼ ounces (35g). Because millions of cans are made, this change means a huge saving in metal.

Similarly, making steel ready for can making now takes 25 percent less energy than it did a decade ago. Among the new technologies that are enabling industry to recycle more economically is the electric arc furnace, a highly efficient, energy-saving method of transforming scrap metal into steel. Also, brewers and carbonated beverage manufacturers have found ways of conserving energy on their can-filling conveyors. Can shapes have been altered to conserve metal. Reducing the diameter of a can at the end (known as "necking in") saves materials. As with thickness, a tiny saving of material in making one can adds up to a huge saving of materials worldwide. Finally, in the can-making process, when parts of a can are stamped out of a coil of metal, all the scrap is now recycled by the industry. All these developments make economic sense and represent a great conservation achievement.

Lightweighting

1970

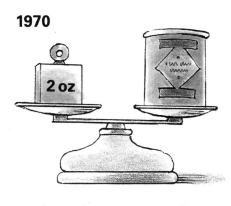

1990

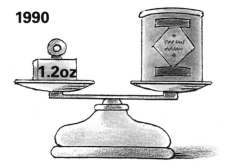

Cans are now made with much thinner walls. This considerably reduces the amount of metal required for their manufacture.

A waste metal processing plant at Hartlepool in the north of England. Here tin is removed, leaving good-quality scrap steel for reuse.

The can makers pay for the recycling of all types of cans through refunding programs. Supermarkets and grocery stores, as well as local authorities, place refund collection bins where large numbers of the public are likely to pass. People are asked to save all kinds of cans and deposit them in the bins. Aluminum and tinplate cans are separated Aluminum cans are sent on to aluminum secondary smelters and the others are de-tinned.

Saving a can aids charity and conserves raw materials.

Producing three-piece cans at AHI Metal Containers in Aukland, New Zealand.

WHERE THE ACTION IS: THEY RECYCLE

Throughout Europe, metal collection points and removal services are common. In Switzerland, there are special collection bins for aluminum and for food tins. The town of Freiburg has recently introduced a system of waste containers for all useful materials. These are known as "green bins" and householders are asked to deposit all recyclable items which are then collected and sorted. Of the waste collected in 1989, 8 percent was scrap metal.

In a "cash for cans" program people pay a deposit added to the price of every can purchased; and this deposit is returned to them when they take the can back for recycling. Some United States can makers and some state legislatures believe this is or would be an ineffective and expensive operation: the costs are passed on directly to the consumer, through rising prices of canned food and drink. However, a "cash for cans" scheme works well in Sweden, where more cans are made of aluminum, which has a higher scrap value than steel.

A European Economic Community (EEC) directive on liquid containers specifies that there shall be no legislation to impose a

Examples of Deposit Laws

STATE	EFFECTIVE DATE	
Connecticut	January, 1980	Minimum $.05 deposit Container handling fee: soft drink=$.02; beer=$.01 Bans sale of detachable pull-tabs on beverage containers
Delaware	July, 1982	Minimum $.05 deposit Minimum 20 percent handling fee Bans detachable pull-tabs on beverage containers Provides for the establishment of redemption centers
Maine	January, 1979	Minimum $.05 deposit Minimum $.02 handling fee Bans detachable pull-tabs on beverage containers Bans nonbiodegradable plastic containers
New York	September, 1983	Minimum $.05 deposit Minimum one-and-a-half cent handling fee Bans detachable pull-tabs on beverage containers Bans plastic secondary packaging that is not photodegradable or biodegradable Provides for the establishment of redemption centers Requires that bottlers pick up empty containers from retailers and pay handling fee within the same credit arrangement as the sale of full goods Requires bottlers to report amount of unclaimed deposits to the state as the Commissioner deems necessary
Vermont	January, 1975	Minimum $.05 deposit Minimum 40 percent handling fee Bans detachable pull-tabs on beverage containers Provides for the establishment of redemption centers Bans plastic or nonbiodegradable "connecting devices"

Individuals have a key role to play in recycling. This young citizen has collected and sorted cans as well as bottles, ready for curbside collection in a community program established in Ohio.

Recycling often means innovation. In Kenya, oil lamps have been made out of old cans.

deposit system, and suggests that voluntary programs are more desirable and effective. Deposit legislation is a part of life for many consumers in the United States. The state of Oregon, for example, passed a bottle bill in 1972, putting a deposit on beverage cans. Shortly after this, Oregon's litter increased by 12 percent and consumers had to pay around 22 percent more for their drinks, not including the returnable deposit. This evidence, together with a report from New York, supports the view that deposit legislation is not effective.

Most states have approached recycling by seeking voluntary contributions. Results have been excellent: Americans are recycling more aluminum cans than ever before (55 percent). The programs include giving donations to charity and so millions of dollars have been received by worthwhile organizations. Many recycling programs in the United States are based on a mixture of methods, including door-to-door collections, central collections and mechanical extraction from waste.

The city of San Jose, California, is but one example of success. One of the largest and most sophisticated multi-material processing centers in California opened there in 1986. Residents place recyclable materials in special containers provided by the city at the side of the street in a "curbside program." These containers are regularly emptied and the contents delivered to the processing plant for weighing and sorting, and are then sold. Metal cans (separated from paper and glass) are conveyed along a sorting line where contaminants are removed, then a magnet separates the steel from the aluminum. The average participating household recycles some 550 pounds (249 kg) of solid waste a year, including 8.1 lb (3.7kg) of tin and 4.2 lb (1.9kg) of aluminum. The director of the San Jose Office of Environmental Management says that: "The curbside recycling program is an integral part of the City Council's adopted integrated waste management strategy. It will be the single most important factor in helping the city keep garbage rates affordable in the long run."

WHERE THE ACTION CAN BE: YOU RECYCLE

your local government and ask if your area has a recycling program. If not, encourage people to do something about starting one.

Recycling cans takes very little time and effort. There are two simple rules for preparing used cans: rinse them out when you have finished doing the dishes (use the dish-wash water to conserve fresh water supplies!) and then squash them. Squashed cans take up far less space, both for you to store them before taking them for recycling and within the collection bin itself. An added advantage is that your garbage can without the tin cans will have much more room for other waste.

The success of large-scale ventures like the San Jose curbside program still depends on individual commitment. Each and every one of us can take action. Recycling begins at home. Look out for community recycling centers and can drop-off locations. Contact

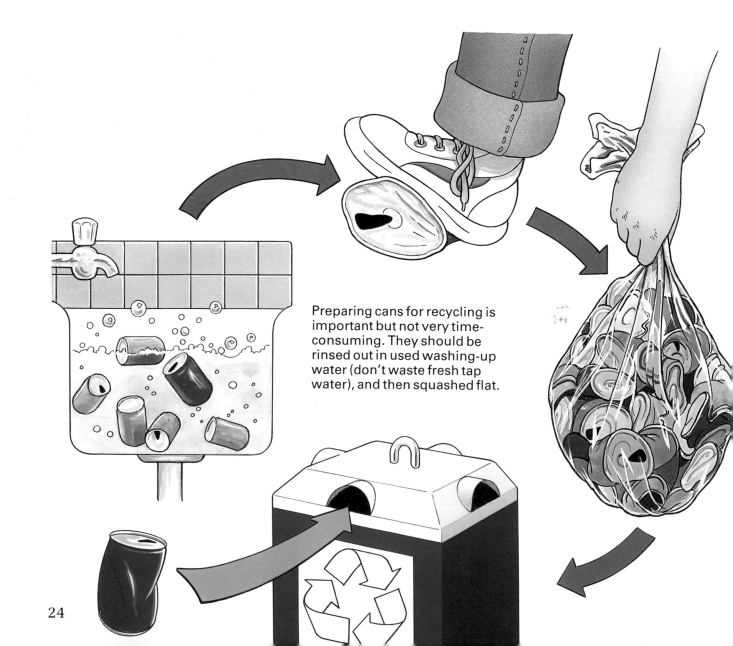

Preparing cans for recycling is important but not very time-consuming. They should be rinsed out in used washing-up water (don't waste fresh tap water), and then squashed flat.

One can will have a lonely journey — and will cost a lot of gasoline money to deliver!

At this collection point in Hampshire, England, consumers are encouraged to "feed the green machine" with used aluminum cans.

Make sure that you deposit your cans safely at the collection point. If money is paid, it will be for those IN the bin, not for those on the ground. Guard against litter at all costs. If the bin is full, the only sensible action is to be patient and bring your cans back another day.

As well as personally delivering cans, enquire about door-to-door collections. If these are not organized by the local government, private organizations may be prepared to collect used metal goods from you. Keep aluminum cans separate from steel ones (use a magnet to tell them apart), as aluminum scrap fetches a higher price than steel.

Metal cans are likely to remain a feature of our lives. The can makers commissioned a research study into attitudes about the packaging of drinks. It showed that cans are associated with good quality and good flavor; they are thought to be better insulators than plastic and cartons, thus keeping their contents cool for a longer time. The can's image also seems important: according to the can makers' study, young people think it looks trendy to be seen with a can, and some adults claim to enjoy their beer at home from cans. Finally, consumers emphasized the convenience of cans. It is to be hoped that such enthusiasm for canned goods will continue into enthusiasm for dealing thoughtfully with the empty cans.

Remember that metal recycling goes beyond the drink can. Look for opportunities to recycle other aluminum goods (for instance, foil, trays, food containers) and never thoughtlessly dispose of household goods that are made of valuable and recyclable metals. Your local government will always advise on the collection of "any old iron and steel."

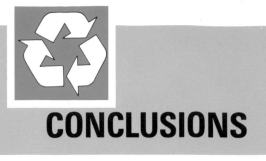

CONCLUSIONS

Individual action plus industrial commitment is a powerful force in the development of worthwhile recycling programs, but action must go hand in hand with information, development and research. Research and development are constantly being undertaken in the metal industry. Recent steps forward in technology have opened up new options for more economic recycling of steel. New techniques allow better use of natural resources, decrease energy consumption and reduce waste. Throughout the world, the industry is committed to good resource management, taking account of both costs and ecological principles.

Such major developments in large industries may seem very remote from individual people and everyday life. But we all need to receive basic information about waste management and recycling so that we understand the need for action and how to get involved. The various organizations and resources listed on page 28 will provide further information about recycling in general or of metals in particular. Also consult your local government and ask in the community. Here are some useful questions to ask:

★ How is solid waste collection/management organized?
★ Who is responsible for the management of waste?
★ What is the local budget for solid waste management?
★ What is the composition of waste in your neighborhood?

Remember, individual action is an essential part of the world's recycling initiatives. These young citizens set the example.

Recycling can indeed be innovative as well as a responsibility. These children in the Sudan are enjoying toy cars that have been made out of metal scrap collected locally.

★ How much of the waste is placed in landfills?
★ Where is the landfill that your community's waste goes to?
★ Does your community have an incinerator?
★ Does your community have a recycling program?
★ Are there door-to-door collections?
★ Where are the collection points?

You could even start a recycling program yourself. Contact your local government for advice. You might also write to industries that benefit from recycling, such as the Aluminum Association and the Institute of Scrap Recycling Industries (see page 28).

As well as taking individual action toward recycling, we can all encourage our local communities to adopt recycling measures and to consider large-scale programs. Underpinning all of this are the essential reasons for reducing waste as a whole:

★ To extend the earth's energy resources
★ To extend the earth's mineral resources
★ To reduce the pollution associated with industry and energy use
★ To reduce environmental/ecological problems related to the disposal of waste

With combined understanding and action from industry and individuals, a great deal can be achieved in terms of making metal a beneficial rather than a problematic part of our world.

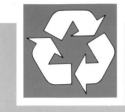

GLOSSARY

RESOURCES

blast furnace large furnace in which iron is extracted from raw materials

corrosion wearing away by chemical action

ferrous containing iron

finite resources resources available in a limited supply, for example, coal and oil. One day we may have used them all

impurities "foreign" matter, causing a substance not to be pure

pollute to make dirty, foul or unclean

recycling the conversion of waste into a reusable product

waste that which is left over after use, superfluous, no longer serving a purpose

For further reading and information (send a stamped, self-addressed envelope for details of costs).

1) *Recycling: Treasure in Our Trash.* A description of recycling and its role in solid waste management, free from National Solid Waste Management Association, 1730 Rhode Island Ave., NW, Washington, DC 20036.

2) *Waste: Choices for Communities.* A citizen's guide to waste disposal practices and the local benefits of recycling. $3 from Concern, Inc. (etc.)

3) The U.S. Environmental Protection Agency also has several recycling publications. Write to 401 M Street, SW, Washington, DC 20460.

4) A variety of pamphlets can be requested from the Toronto Recycling Committee, 1 Dundas Street West, Suite 2602, Toronto, Ontario M5G 1Z3.

ADDRESSES

Aluminum Association, 818 Connecticut Avenue, NW, Washington, DC 200006

Aluminum Recycling Association, 900 Seventeen Street, NW, Suite 504, Washington, DC 20006

Environmental Defense Fund, 1616 P Street, NW, Washington, DC 20036

Greenpeace, USA, 1611 Connecticut Avenue, NW, Washington, DC 20009

Institute of Scrap Recycling Industries, Inc., 1627 K Street, NW, Suite 700, Washington, DC 20006

Pollution Probe, 12 Madison Avenue, Toronto, Ontario M5R 2S1, Canada

U.S. Environmental Protection Agency, 401 M Street, SW, Washington, DC 20460

World Watch Institute, 1776 Massachusetts Avenue, NW, Washington, DC 20036

INDEX

PRINTED IN BELGIUM BY

INTERNATIONAL BOOK PRODUCTION